HOWARD BRENTON

Howard Brenton was born in Portsmouth in 1942. His many plays include *Christie in Love* (Portable Theatre, 1969); *Revenge* (Theatre Upstairs, 1969); *Magnificence* (Royal Court Theatre, 1973); *The Churchill Play* (Nottingham Playhouse, 1974, and twice revived by the RSC, 1978 and 1988); *Bloody Poetry* (Foco Novo, 1984, and Royal Court Theatre, 1987); *Weapons of Happiness* (National Theatre, Evening Standard Award, 1976); *Epsom Downs* (Joint Stock Theatre, 1977); *Sore Throats* (RSC, 1978); *The Romans in Britain* (National Theatre, 1980, revived at the Crucible Theatre, Sheffield, 2006); *Thirteenth Night* (RSC, 1981); *The Genius* (1983), *Greenland* (1988) and *Berlin Bertie* (1992), all presented by the Royal Court; *Kit's Play* (RADA Jerwood Theatre, 2000); *Paul* (National Theatre, 2005); *In Extremis* (Shakespeare's Globe, 2006 and 2007); *Never So Good* (National Theatre, 2008); *The Ragged Trousered Philanthropists* adapted from the novel by Robert Tressell (Liverpool Everyman and Chichester Festival Theatre, 2010); *Anne Boleyn* (Shakespeare's Globe, 2010 and 2011); *55 Days* (Hampstead Theatre, 2012); *#aiww: The Arrest of Ai Weiwei* (Hampstead Theatre, 2013); *The Guffin* (NT Connections, 2013); *Drawing the Line* (Hampstead Theatre, 2013) and *Doctor Scroggy's War* (Shakespeare's Globe, 2014).

Collaborations with other writers include *Brassneck* (with David Hare, Nottingham Playhouse, 1972); *Pravda* (with David Hare, National Theatre, Evening Standard Award, 1985) and *Moscow Gold* (with Tariq Ali, RSC, 1990).

Versions of classics include *The Life of Galileo* (1980) and *Danton's Death* (1982) both for the National Theatre, Goethe's *Faust* (1995/6) for the RSC, a new version of *Danton's Death* for the National Theatre (2010) and *Dances of Death* (Gate Theatre, 2013).

He wrote thirteen episodes of the BBC1 drama series *Spooks* (2001–05, BAFTA Best Drama Series, 2003).

Other Titles from Nick Hern Books

Howard Brenton

LAWRENCE
AFTER ARABIA

NICK HERN BOOKS
London
www.nickhernbooks.co.uk

A Nick Hern Book

Lawrence After Arabia first published in Great Britain as a paperback original in 2016 by Nick Hern Books Limited, The Glasshouse, 49a Goldhawk Road, London W12 8QP

Lawrence After Arabia copyright © 2016 Howard Brenton

Howard Brenton has asserted his right to be identified as the author of this work

Excerpts from *Saint Joan* by George Bernard Shaw reproduced with kind permission by The Society of Authors, on behalf of the Bernard Shaw Estate

Cover image copyright © The Granger Collection/Topfoto/ArenaPAL

Designed and typeset by Nick Hern Books, London
Printed in the UK by Mimeo Ltd, Huntingdon, Cambridgeshire PE29 6XX

A CIP catalogue record for this book is available from the British Library

ISBN 978 1 84842 577 4

Lawrence After Arabia was first performed at Hampstead Theatre, London, on 28 April 2016, with the following cast:

LOWELL THOMAS	Sam Alexander
FIELD MARSHAL EDMUND ALLENBY	William Chubb
CHARLOTTE SHAW	Geraldine James
PRINCE FEISAL	Khalid Laith
T.E. LAWRENCE	Jack Laskey
BLANCHE PATCH	Rosalind March
GEORGE BERNARD SHAW	Jeff Rawle

Director	John Dove
Designer	Michael Taylor
Lighting	Mark Doubleday
Sound	John Leonard
Composer	Philip Pinsky
Casting	Crowley Poole

Characters

BLANCHE PATCH, *forty-three years*
GEORGE BERNARD SHAW, *sixty-six years*
CHARLOTTE PAYNE-TOWNSHEND SHAW, *sixty-three years*
LOWELL THOMAS, *thirty years*
T.E. LAWRENCE, *'Tom' to his friends, thirty-four years*
PRINCE FEISAL, *thirty-eight years*
FIELD MARSHAL EDMUND ALLENBY, *fifty-four years*

Setting

The action takes place at Shaw's Corner, the home of George Bernard and Charlotte Shaw, in the Hertfordshire village of Ayot St Lawrence, in August 1922 and February 1923, and in the head of T.E. Lawrence.

Author's Note

T.E. Lawrence and George Bernard Shaw are 'Tom' and 'GBS' in speech prefixes, but 'Lawrence' and 'Shaw' in stage directions. I wanted to use the personal names of the principal characters when they are speaking, but in the stage directions I don't want readers to lose sight of their fame.

H.B.

This text went to press before the end of rehearsals and so may differ slightly from the play as performed.

ACT ONE

Scene One

August 1922. CHARLOTTE's sitting room at Shaw's Corner, Ayot St Lawrence. The windows are opened out onto an expansive lawn, trees and bushes and fields beyond.

BLANCHE PATCH *sits on a sofa, pen in hand, paper on a board on her lap. She is still.*

Nothing happens.

GEORGE BERNARD SHAW – GBS – *enters at speed. He stops. He raises a hand dramatically to say something. He freezes.*

After a lengthy pause he turns and exits at speed.

PATCH *sighs then is still.*

CHARLOTTE PAYNE-TOWNSHEND SHAW, *married to* SHAW, *enters at speed.*

CHARLOTTE. Has he…?

PATCH *shakes her head.*

CHARLOTTE *sighs and exits.*

Nothing happens.

SHAW *enters.*

GBS. Where were we?

PATCH. 'The records of the Holy Inquisition…'

GBS. Ah. Yes. Very fine.

He stares. He raises an arm as if to speak rhetorically. He freezes. Then he turns and exits at speed.

And immediately re-enters, raises his arm and declaims.
PATCH *is writing at speed – shorthand.*

The records of the Holy Inquisition are full of histories we dare not give to the world, because they are beyond the belief of honest men and innocent women; yet they all began with saintly simpletons.

He pauses then lowers his arm.

Saintly simpletons. I like to think I am not one of them. I do play the fool from time to time, to annoy people. After all, I am a playwright.

He laughs. PATCH *has written the last comment down.*

No, Patch, that is not in the speech.

PATCH. But you spoke it.

GBS. The Grand Inquisitor is not a playwright.

PATCH. For all I know you may have decided to make him one.

GBS. Why, on this sweet and good earth, would I do that?

PATCH. There have been greater nonsenses in your plays than playwrighting Grand Inquisitors.

GBS. 'Nonsenses'? Patch, after all your years as my secretary, are you turning critic?

PATCH. I am not being critical. I am being objective.

GBS. That's what the scoundrels always say.

PATCH. You were a critic for many years.

GBS. Only because I needed the money. Where were we?

PATCH. Saintly simpletons.

GBS. Yes.

He pauses and raises his arm. He is about to declaim but CHARLOTTE *enters at speed.*

CHARLOTTE. He is American.

GBS. Who is?

CHARLOTTE. You know who. And he's been sitting in the hall for an hour. Americans hate waiting.

GBS. Advise him to shrug off his national characteristics and prepare for bitter disappointment. I speak as an Irishman.

CHARLOTTE. Don't be so knobbly. You agreed to see him.

GBS. Patch, please buy me a railway ticket.

PATCH. To where?

GBS. Crewe Station. It has an excellent tea room. I have written some of my best work in railway tea rooms, they are temples of perfect peace. Oh, very well, let us graciously grant audience to our American cousin.

CHARLOTTE, *leaving*.

Knobbly?

She turns.

CHARLOTTE. Very much.

GBS. As what?

CHARLOTTE. Your old walking stick?

GBS. I was thinking more: knobbly as a great oak in the forest?

CHARLOTTE (*shaking her head*). Old walking stick.

CHARLOTTE *exits, smiling*.

PATCH. Do you want me to type up the speech?

GBS. No no, it's not done yet. I fear the Grand Inquisitor has much more to say.

PATCH. I will bicycle to Harpenden and purchase your railway ticket.

GBS. I was joking.

PATCH. You know I can never tell what is a joke with you and what is not.

She is going.

GBS. Patch, do you know why you are so invaluable to me?

PATCH. My skill at using your system of shorthand dictation?

GBS. You refuse to be my audience.

PATCH. I'm just not artistic.

She exits.

SHAW *alone. He paces. He stops.*

GBS. Heresy. Yes. Must get the speech onto heresy.

Rhetorical stance, arm raised.

'Heresy at first seems innocent and even laudable; but it ends in such a monstrous horror of unnatural wickedness that the most tender-hearted amongst you, if you saw it at work...' Or something like. The Grand Inquisitor as a playwright? (*Laughs.*) Twisting the plot upside down? Making the Church not the tyrannical, torturing organisation it was, but... merciful? Tip the world over, see what falls out...

CHARLOTTE (*off*). If you would like to come into my sitting room?

THOMAS (*off*). Your house is charming, Mrs Shaw.

CHARLOTTE (*off*). Why thank you, Mr Thomas.

GBS. Public Man! Go!

CHARLOTTE *and* LOWELL THOMAS, *American, enter.*

My dear Mr Thomas, welcome to Shaw's Corner.

THOMAS. Mr Shaw, it is a great honour to meet you.

GBS. Not at all. I have to meet myself every day and I assure you it is... nothing special. Please...

He gestures, they sit.

Forgive me for having to make you wait, I was detained by the Inquisition.

THOMAS. So it's true? You're writing a play about St Joan?

GBS. I have heard that rumour. Sometimes I believe it, sometimes not.

THOMAS. May I publish a hint?

GBS. My dear Thomas, it would be folly for a mere playwright to attempt to manipulate the press.

THOMAS. Really? When you were young, didn't you write articles about your own plays? Under false names?

GBS. Only to attack myself. Someone had to do it.

THOMAS. Please, don't misunderstand me. I admire the way you struggled. Getting noticed is the first duty of an artist. I say communicate or die.

GBS. Mmm. The single biggest problem with communication is the illusion that it has taken place.

THOMAS *is momentarily stumped by this*.

A pause.

Mint tea?

THOMAS....Excellent.

CHARLOTTE. It's the maid's day off, let me…

She is about to stand but SHAW *is on his feet before her.*

GBS. I will make it.

CHARLOTTE. Crush the leaves.

GBS. As you know, my dear, I prefer to tear them.

CHARLOTTE. If you tear the leaves, half the mintiness is already on your fingers.

GBS. On the contrary, the mintiness is released. (*To* THOMAS.) There is also carrot cake.

He grins and exits at speed.

CHARLOTTE. The pleasures of domesticity, Mr Thomas. Are you married?

THOMAS. Frances is devoted to me. She has to be, particularly as I am a traveller, much in the world.

CHARLOTTE. Indeed? (*A beat.*) Forgive me for being blunt. But I do believe I know why you are here.

THOMAS. Perhaps we should wait until Mr Shaw…

CHARLOTTE. He does intend to make tea but he is writing a play and is easily diverted. He has a writing hut at the bottom of the garden. And he can disappear altogether to railway stations.

THOMAS. Ah.

A pause.

CHARLOTTE. You are here about Colonel Lawrence.

THOMAS. Yes.

CHARLOTTE. Shaw and I were at the Covent Garden Theatre for your lecture.

THOMAS. I did peek through the curtain to see your arrival in the stalls. The audience stood and applauded.

CHARLOTTE. My husband knows all about entrances.

THOMAS. I did have hopes that you and Mr Shaw would come backstage.

CHARLOTTE. Please be reassured, we very much enjoyed the evening.

THOMAS. Well, good.

A pause.

CHARLOTTE. Perhaps your title was a little brash.

THOMAS. 'Brash'?

CHARLOTTE. 'Lawrence Hero of Arabia As I Knew Him.'

THOMAS. Well, he is a hero and I did know him.

CHARLOTTE. You did give the impression that had there been water in the desert, Colonel Lawrence would have walked upon it.

THOMAS. You have to popularise, Mrs Shaw. You have to hammer home. The lectures are for the general public, which is huge.

CHARLOTTE. And you did hugely generalise.

THOMAS. May I blow my trumpet?

CHARLOTTE. As loud as you wish.

THOMAS. Without my photographs, my articles in the press both sides of the Atlantic, my lecture tour, without me, would the world know anything about 'Lawrence of Arabia'?

CHARLOTTE. One is tempted to reply: can one really know anything at all about him? I find Tom Lawrence an enigma, even after reading his manuscript.

THOMAS. Manuscript?

CHARLOTTE. The *Seven Pillars of Wisdom*.

THOMAS. You've read the *Seven Pillars*?

CHARLOTTE. Lawrence asked Shaw to edit it. He's made a start but heaven knows when he'll finish.

THOMAS. You have the *Seven Pillars of Wisdom* in this house? (*Looks around.*) In this room?

CHARLOTTE. I gather you have not read it.

THOMAS. No. Yes. Not actually… no. He told me he lost it on a railway station in a place called Reading.

CHARLOTTE. He did. What is it about men in my life and railway stations?

THOMAS. So there was another copy…

CHARLOTTE. Oh no. Lawrence sat down and wrote it all out again. In six weeks. Then gave it to us.

THOMAS (*losing his temper*). I am sick and tired of this treatment! I was there with him in Arabia. If anyone is to edit his goddamn book, it should be me!

CHARLOTTE. Mr Thomas, language.

THOMAS. I am badly dealt with. Very badly. Lawrence agreed
to appear at my lectures. Has he turned up, even once? No.
And next week we are meant to leave for the States! All he
has to do is simply appear. Not speak, not take questions, just
stand there. You know, in the robes.

CHARLOTTE. Not on a camel?

THOMAS. Animals are difficult on tour.

CHARLOTTE. What do you want me to do, Mr Thomas?

THOMAS. Tell me where he is.

CHARLOTTE. You mean you have lost him?

THOMAS. He disappeared from his lodgings four weeks ago.

CHARLOTTE. Really?

THOMAS. Where is the so-called uncrowned King of Arabia,
Mrs Shaw?

CHARLOTTE. I have not the faintest idea, Mr Thomas.

THOMAS. I don't believe you.

A silence.

CHARLOTTE. Well, you are going to have to.

THOMAS. Is he here? Are you hiding him? Is he at the top of
the house, right now?

CHARLOTTE. Thank you very much for calling, Mr Thomas.

CHARLOTTE *stands.*

THOMAS. You have got to know where he is.

For a moment he stays seated, then he stands.

There is a cost to fame, Mrs Shaw. It is people like me.

CHARLOTTE. Yes. Success is a swamp, full of leeches.

He glares at her.

THOMAS. I could give another lecture. About a wholly
different Lawrence in the desert, the hot, filthy dirt of the

desert. I could tell you hot, filthy, dirty brutal private things, about your brilliant friend. The cosy furniture in this room would blush, more than blush, catch fire, burn down into ash. Along with his reputation and those who support him.

She glares at him.

CHARLOTTE. Allow me to show you out.

THOMAS. No need. I am not going to snoop in your cupboards for war heroes.

CHARLOTTE. Good day, Mr Thomas.

THOMAS. Good day, Mrs Shaw.

He exits.

For a moment CHARLOTTE *stands still. Then she sits and is shaking.*

A pause.

SHAW *enters.*

GBS. Better late than never, the mint is stewing… (*Stops.*) What have you done with our American?

CHARLOTTE. I sent him packing.

GBS. My dear, what is the matter?

CHARLOTTE. When did you last hear from Tom?

GBS. Four, five weeks ago?

CHARLOTTE. The American says he's disappeared.

GBS. Tom is an adventurer. Adventurers disappear into… thickets, woods, deserts.

CHARLOTTE. I'm worried, Bernard.

GBS. Don't be. He'll turn up. Lawrence is forever backing into the limelight.

Scene Two

The room and the garden, empty. The windows still open.

A glissando-like sound.

The sunlight shifts.

Then T.E. LAWRENCE – TOM – *enters at the back of the garden, pushes through bushes. He wears an RAF uniform – Aircraftsman Second Class.*

He stands on the lawn looking into the house.

CHARLOTTE *enters, carrying a bulky manuscript. At first she does not see* LAWRENCE. *She turns and does. A sharp intake of breath.*

They look at each other, both still.

CHARLOTTE. Good morning.

TOM. Good morning.

CHARLOTTE. Can I help you...?

A pause.

Tom?

TOM. Hello, Charlotte, my dear. Forgive me for using the back gate. One never knows whether journalists are lurking at one's friends' front doors.

CHARLOTTE. Tom! Oh dear God.

She exits at speed. LAWRENCE *laughs and – perfectly at ease – walks into the room. He looks at the manuscript on the table, turns a page.*

CHARLOTTE *enters with* SHAW. *They look at the relaxed* LAWRENCE.

GBS. In the name of sanity, man, why are you dressed like that?

TOM. The blue? Actually you begin the training in khaki, which is horrible.

CHARLOTTE. Training?

TOM. Yes. I've enlisted in the RAF.

A pause.

GBS. You have done what?

CHARLOTTE. You're a colonel in the Army. Why do you want to be an RAF officer?

TOM. Oh, I'm not an officer, I'm an Aircraftsman Second Class. A raw recruit. (*Grins.*) The lowest of the low.

He touches the manuscript on the table.

My book! It's what I want to talk to you about.

GBS. Tom, you are very well aware of the shock you've given us. Unexpected entrances are always fun. But could you please sit down and allow your audience to adjust?

TOM. Of course. If there is carrot cake.

GBS. There will be carrot cake hereafter.

TOM. Oh good.

LAWRENCE *sits, an arm casually across the back of the armchair.*

CHARLOTTE. Enlisted in the RAF.

TOM. I'm doing basic training at a depot in Uxbridge.

CHARLOTTE. How is that possible?

TOM. Well, it's not easy, the other recruits are ten years younger than I. But I think I'm up to it physically.

CHARLOTTE. No...

GBS. How in heaven's name can you enlist as a squaddie in the RAF when you are Colonel Thomas Edward Lawrence, late of Arabia?

TOM. Oh, no one knows who I am at Uxbridge, I didn't enlist under my own name, of course not. I'm like Odysseus. You

know: when he told the Cyclops his name was 'No One'.
So when I'm asked I say 'No One'. And no one sees me.
Or that's the desired effect.

A grin.

GBS. So what name are you using?

TOM. John Hume Ross.

GBS. Ross.

TOM. Good, isn't it, I wanted something anonymous. A no name for no one.

GBS. I fear it will not be anonymous for long.

CHARLOTTE. Yes, Tom, surely, people will recognise you. I mean, how did you get here?

TOM. I took the train to Harpenden then walked.

GBS. And no one spotted you?

TOM. Why should they? Lawrence of Arabia wears desert robes, not this… (*Touches his clothes.*) All people see is a uniform. I was sitting in a working-man's café the other day. Above my head on the wall there was a picture of me in the desert. No one made the connection. It's so wonderful being invisible. At times when I see my hands on a table, I think I can see right through them. You're my best friends, you will keep my secret, won't you?

CHARLOTTE. Of course, Tom, without question.

SHAW *stands.*

GBS. I'll speak to the servants. They're well-trained, we've had all sorts undercover here: Prime Ministers, film stars. Though none of them as high in the public's league of fame as you, my dear fellow. And you must eat more than cake, you're a scarecrow.

He exits.

Awkward moment.

TOM. My dear Charlotte. How are you? The…

CHARLOTTE. My arthritis? It rages through me.

TOM. Is there nothing…

CHARLOTTE. Oh, painkillers, morphine. But I refuse to take them. I hate their invasion of the mind.

TOM. Yes. Clarity of mind is the most precious thing we have. Unfortunately it's not often with us.

CHARLOTTE. No.

A moment.

What are you doing, Tom?

TOM. I'm changing into someone else.

CHARLOTTE. And your mind is clear?

TOM. Absolutely.

CHARLOTTE. Into someone else? Why?

TOM. Isn't that obvious? I don't want to be me.

CHARLOTTE. But you're a man of great achievements, a soldier, a wonderful writer, like a… like a modern knight.

TOM. A knight? Is that how you see me?

CHARLOTTE. The whole country does.

TOM. I'll tell you what I really want to be. Lower than the lowest of the low.

CHARLOTTE. And how are you getting on with that?

TOM. It's a work in progress. Yesterday I was on the shit cart.

CHARLOTTE. The…

TOM. The latrines at the barracks are not on the public sewers. There are pits that have to be dug out. It's a punishment detail, I find myself on it rather a lot. There's a drill sergeant who is determined to break me, he thinks I'm some kind of pansy.

CHARLOTTE. Tom, that's horrible.

TOM. Don't worry. I will break him.

CHARLOTTE. How will you do that?…

TOM. Words, I'll use words. My fellow recruits love a bit of cheek at the NCOs. I'll choose my moment, it may cost me a week on the shit cart but it will be worth it.

He grins.

CHARLOTTE. How do you get on with the other men?

He looks at her for a moment.

TOM. What do you know about the working classes?

CHARLOTTE. We're socialists.

TOM. Yes, but what do you know about them?

CHARLOTTE. Bernard has written a lot for the Fabian Society on social conditions…

TOM. Yes, but do you really know what they are *like*? No offence, Charlotte, but you're from a rich middle-class family.

CHARLOTTE. Well, perhaps one is a little limited.

TOM. I found them a profound shock. I was a loner in the Army, with the Intelligence Corps in Cairo. I've never known barracks life, until now.

CHARLOTTE. Do they… accept you?

TOM. At first they called me 'Pear Drops'.

CHARLOTTE. Pear drops?

TOM. Because of my accent. They said I speak as if I've got sweets in my mouth.

CHARLOTTE. I see. (*Catches herself.*) Do we all…?

LAWRENCE *laughs.*

TOM. Recently they've begun to call me 'Professor'. I write love letters to their girls for them, I use bits of Shakespeare's sonnets and Catullus. They copy them out in their own hand, of course. Though not all of them can write well. And some of them are rough – the other night two of them had a go at me.

CHARLOTTE. A go...?

TOM. Tried to beat me up. They'd taken against me reading Greek at night. Fortunately I've got a protector, a brute of a Scot who's taken a shine to me. It's all really like a farmyard, once you know where you are in the pecking order, you're fine.

CHARLOTTE. Tom, why are you doing this? Do you want to destroy yourself?

TOM. Destroy this self, yes, why not? Reinvent myself. Strip down. Find a death in life, bury myself and then... really come alive. Finally be... real. (*Taking her hand.*) Oh, Charlotte, I so want you to understand.

CHARLOTTE. And I want to, but you're wrapping yourself up in a mystery.

TOM. I'm not. It's simple: I just want to be... normal.

CHARLOTTE. Well, that really is a mystery. Don't talk to Bernard like this. To him mysteries are false beasts to be hunted down by jokes.

TOM. Yes.

Enter SHAW. *He carries a leather suitcase, much battered but of great quality.*

GBS. All are sworn to silence, conspiracy grips the house. Mrs Higgs is preparing a mighty nut roast with our very own purple sprouting broccoli. A bed is ready for you, you can stay?

TOM. Tonight. I have a weekend pass. But I must be back in Uxbridge on Monday morning.

GBS. Excellent. And, if you remember, you left this with us for safe keeping, two years ago.

He puts the suitcase down. LAWRENCE *glances at it then looks away.*

A pause.

TOM. What I'm really here about is my book.

CHARLOTTE. Yes, I've been reading it too and…

TOM. I don't want to publish it.

GBS. But it's a masterpiece.

TOM. That's the trouble. It's too literary, too artistic. I want to cut it down, make a popular book. For the general reader.

CHARLOTTE. So you're not entirely giving up public life.

TOM. I just want the Arabs' story told. I owe it to them. (*To* SHAW.) Will you help me with the editing?

GBS. I am writing *Saint Joan*. Unfortunately that too is a masterpiece, so my time…

CHARLOTTE. I'll do it.

They look at her.

It will help me to understand.

GBS. That's settled then! Tom, you'll work here. Whenever you can get leave from your pit of self-imposed suffering. Forgive me if I leave you now. There is something of a crisis at the bottom of the garden: The Spanish Inquisition is occupying my writing hut.

He strides off down the garden and exits.

TOM. Writing hut?

CHARLOTTE. Yes, it's his new contraption, didn't you see it in the bushes? It is on a sort of revolving platform, so the windows can follow the sun. It has a table, a chair, a typewriter and a bed.

TOM. What more does a writer need?

CHARLOTTE. Well…

A pause.

This is going to be such fun. You must tell me all about meeting Prince Feisal. He sounds a wonderful man.

A beat.

TOM. Yes.

A pause.

Feisal.

Enter PATCH.

PATCH. Would you like to see your room, Colonel Lawrence?

TOM. Yes… thank you…

PATCH. It's at the back of the house, journalists won't be able to see you.

TOM. Well, good.

He hesitates, then follows her.

CHARLOTTE is alone. She realises he has not taken the suitcase. She is about to call out but does not.

She looks at the suitcase.

She runs her hands across the leather.

She puts her thumbs on the latches. She clicks them open. She is about to open the case. But thinks better of it and clicks it shut.

Scene Three

The room. Moonlight.

LAWRENCE *enters. He is barefoot and in long johns. He tiptoes.*

He looks at the suitcase. He is still. Then he goes to it. Opens it, and takes out the army uniform of a lieutenant.

Then he takes out Arab robes.

He lays both sets of clothes across the table. He looks at them, he crouches down, hugging himself.

TOM. Feisal.

He stands. He lifts the army uniform and caresses it.

To meet a Prince, for the sake of England.

He sits abruptly and is pulling on the trousers quickly. Then he puts on socks and shoes.

What is your duty, soldier? My duty is to the badge on the cap, sir. Always salute the badge on the cap, sir. Not the man, no, sir, never the man, sir. We die but the badge lives on, sir. Badge of England. Badge of service. Badge of Empire. Badge of duty. Badge of death. Of...

He is suddenly dead still.

How beautiful with badges.

He laughs at the line of thought and is dressing himself quickly again. Shirt on. Then he lifts the uniform's jacket. He slips it on, does the buttons up, calmly. He finally takes out the hat from the suitcase. He looks at the badge and caresses it with a finger.

Will it never leave me, the desire for what all men want?

He puts the cap on.

Glory.

And the room becomes...

Scene Four

…a colonnaded courtyard in bright sunlight.

LAWRENCE *to the side, as if outside the house.*

Enter FEISAL. *For a moment he is alone.*

Then two FIGHTERS *– in Arab robes and armed – enter. One whispers into* FEISAL*'s ear. (He is telling him that* LAWRENCE *has arrived and is waiting outside.)*

For a while FEISAL *does not react. Then he sighs and waves a hand, meaning 'let him come in'.*

The FIGHTER *goes to* LAWRENCE. *He leads him into the courtyard.*

LAWRENCE *and* FEISAL *look at each other.*

A silence.

FEISAL. So. (*A beat.*) So you are the British officer.

TOM. Yes, Your Highness.

FEISAL. I have heard you have been travelling, visiting members of my family. My father in Mecca, then my three brothers: Emir Abdullah in Jeddah, then Emir Ali and Emir Zeid in Rabegh.

TOM. Yes, Your Highness.

FEISAL. It is a hundred miles from Rabegh. A difficult road.

TOM. My camel is a knowledgeable animal.

FEISAL. A British Army uniform perched on a camel? It's surprising you survived.

TOM. I wrapped myself in a good, Arab cloak.

FEISAL. Ah, a disguise.

TOM. A sensible garment in October.

FEISAL. Though it is still hot in the day, you must have suffered discomfort?

TOM. Not at all.

A very awkward pause.

Your Highness...

FEISAL *raises his hand, sharply.*

FEISAL. What is your name?

TOM. Captain Lawrence.

FEISAL. So, Captain Lawrence, do you like my family house here in Wadi Safra?

TOM. It is not in Damascus.

A silence. This is a dangerous moment.

FEISAL. To live in Damascus, I would first have to kill many Turks.

TOM. Yes.

FEISAL. Which, praise be to God, would be a blessing to the Arab people.

TOM. Yes!

FEISAL. And to the British Empire.

TOM. Your Highness...

Again FEISAL *raises his hand sharply to stop* LAWRENCE. *He gestures to the* FIGHTERS, *who exit.*

FEISAL. You must understand my caution. You are a young man. Your rank in the British Army is not high. But you have been visiting members of my family, one after another, asking them about the Turkish occupation. Why?

TOM. To find the leader who can drive the Turks from Arabia.

FEISAL. My father is the leader of the revolt against the Turks.

TOM. He is a great man, to be much honoured.

FEISAL. Indeed.

TOM. Who would glory to see his son lead the tribes to victory.

A silence.

FEISAL. You have been sent by General Allenby?

TOM. I have sent myself. I am on leave.

FEISAL. Leave.

TOM. Holiday.

FEISAL. Holiday! (*Laughs.*)

TOM. I have come to speak to you, warrior to warrior.

FEISAL. Mm. Then I say to you, 'warrior to warrior', will you give me gold and guns?

TOM. Allenby will give you gold and guns. But I will give you what you really need.

FEISAL. And what is that, Captain Lawrence?

TOM. Military strategy.

FEISAL (*laughs*). The Bedu are a direct people. In war we know one thing: charge, kill, loot and leave.

TOM. Which is a great strategy, in the right place and at the right time.

FEISAL. We will talk.

FEISAL exits.

The scene fading, the house and garden reappearing.

LAWRENCE stumbles back into the living room, tearing off the uniform, throwing it around the floor.

The Arab robes are still laid out on the sofa.

TOM. Strategy.

He crouches down in a huddle. His back is badly scarred. He draws a map, trance-like, on the floor.

I saw you in wartime. Vehicles burning on the skyline, dead animals in the wadis, the massacred by sabotaged railway lines. And I dreamt of the peace. Mesopotamia, dig new irrigation, make Baghdad a city of gardens, unite the tribes, a wonderful country: Palestine to the Persian border, to the Red Sea in the south. And Damascus will be your capital, oh Arabia, my bride, my husband.

He pulls himself into a fetal position, lying on the floor.

CHARLOTTE. Save us all!

She turns her back.

TOM. Charlotte, I do apologise.

He pulls the undergarment robe to him and is pulling it over his head hurriedly.

CHARLOTTE. Too fluffed up?

TOM. What?

CHARLOTTE. The guest bed, too soft?

TOM. No, it's all me...

CHARLOTTE. We can find a hard mattress, I'm sure. I expect you're used to hard rugs on sand...

TOM. There was sand, there were rugs. And fleas.

CHARLOTTE. I don't think we can offer fleas.

TOM. I'm decent now.

She hesitates then turns.

CHARLOTTE. Goodness me.

TOM. They are practical garments.

CHARLOTTE. They must be... very.

TOM. This is the *thobe*... (*Sweeping the overgarment on.*) And this is the cloak, the *bisht*. The headdress... (*Arranges it, then the rope.*) The rope is called an *aqel*, it's made of gold thread and silk. (*Pointing to the neck.*) See the embroidery? These are the clothes of a wealthy man.

CHARLOTTE. You bought them?

TOM. They were a gift from Prince Feisal. Actually, they are a man's wedding garments. His great aunt in Medina sent them to him, I think as a heavy hint. And he... (*Airy gesture.*) passed them on.

CHARLOTTE. How wonderful. Just like the photographs! Though was there a... you know, dagger?

TOM. Someone else has it.

A beat.

CHARLOTTE. Tom... are you in pain?

For a moment he does not understand.

TOM. Oh, the scars! No no, they're nothing.

CHARLOTTE. Actually I don't mean physical pain, I mean spiritual.

TOM. Well... Do you know Oscar Wilde's prayer? 'Dear Lord, if you take away the physical pain, I'll take care of the spiritual.'

He grins.

CHARLOTTE. You can talk to me, you know.

TOM. I know, Charlotte, You're a very good friend.

A silence, they are looking at each other.

CHARLOTTE. Well. Do stay down, if you want. Bernard will be up and doing at six.

TOM. Right.

Another brief moment. Then she turns and exits.

LAWRENCE *turns away, angry with himself.*

The danger of friends.

And the sitting room is dissolving as...

Scene Five

The desert. Sunrise to bright light.

THOMAS *enters. He is dressed somewhat comically in Bermuda shorts, a blanket wrapped round his shoulders, and he is struggling with cumbersome photographic equipment: camera attached to tripod, container with strap for plates, then state-of-the-art flash equipment.*

LAWRENCE *walks into the scene.* THOMAS *concentrates on setting up the tripod, not looking at* LAWRENCE.

THOMAS. Damned inconvenient, the desert. Gritty.

TOM. But excellent for a war.

THOMAS. Not if it's the war you're trying to photograph. Flies in the lens, plates cracking, sand in the developing chemicals.

TOM. The desert's clean. Just you and the enemy. It's like a stage.

THOMAS. Yup! A stage burning at day with clouds of flies as extras, freezing at night with a chorus of bugs to bite you.

TOM. The flies? Kill them!

LAWRENCE *pirouettes and slaps his hands at a fly in the air. The robes swirl. He holds up a palm, grins. Then he looks away.*

The Arabs call the desert the garden of Allah. Because there is no one in it but God.

THOMAS (*low*). And His flies and bugs. (*To* LAWRENCE.) Lawrence, I said: not the robes, not for this shoot.

TOM. Why not?

THOMAS. You can't appear in the London *Times* in a dress.

TOM. Do you have any idea how insulting that is? To me, to the Prince?

THOMAS. You're a British Army Officer, this is meant to be a picture of you and him on the battlefield. You've got to be in uniform.

TOM. This is my uniform now.

He claps his hands at another fly.

Enter FEISAL *with armed* FIGHTERS. *One has a chair.*

FEISAL. Do the camel flies distress you, Lawrence?

He laughs. The FIGHTERS *laugh.*

TOM. No, Your Highness. But maybe you should teach your camels… to teach their flies… to bite Turks, not your friends.

FEISAL *laughs, as do the* FIGHTERS. *The chair is put down and* FEISAL *sits on it as…*

THOMAS. What did he say?

TOM. He said how pleased he is I'm wearing a dress.

THOMAS (*sotto*). Damn Arabic…

FEISAL. Lawrence, I have a gift for you.

He gestures and one of his FIGHTERS *approaches* LAWRENCE *with a curved knife in a scabbard.*

THOMAS (*sotto*). What the…

TOM (*sotto*). Be still.

The FIGHTER *circles* LAWRENCE *then ties the belt around his waist, arranging the robes. He steps back.*

A pause.

Your Highness, I am overcome with gratitude to receive a gift of such splendour.

FEISAL. It's nothing. You can swat the flies with it.

Laughter.

What is your servant doing with that contraption?

TOM. Your Highness, would you permit a photograph?

Unease. THOMAS *is having difficulty with the camera.*

FEISAL. The problem with photographs is: what do they show?

TOM. They will show Your Highness planning a battle.

FEISAL. But I am not planning a battle. I am being amused by your servant's antics.

TOM. We will pose as if we were planning a battle.

FEISAL. I find that unseemly.

TOM. The picture will tell a story. And the King of England will see it.

FEISAL. In *The Times* newspaper? Well, well.

TOM. Yes. The King will see the photograph. I promise Your Highness, it will advance the cause of the Arab revolt.

FEISAL. Promises are dangerous, Lawrence.

He stands suddenly and walks away with a gesture to LAWRENCE *to follow him.*

TOM (*to* THOMAS). Do this later.

THOMAS. But I've set up…

TOM. Just get out of the way, you fool.

THOMAS *is exasperated. The* FIGHTERS *laugh at him.* THOMAS *lugs the equipment away.*

LAWRENCE *and* FEISAL *walk away to speak privately.*

FEISAL. Lawrence, many of the tribal leaders cannot understand why we do not attack Medina.

TOM. Then, Your Highness, I urge you to counsel them.

FEISAL. Never forget, English soldier, Medina is the second home of the Prophet, peace be upon him. My family are seen as the guardians of the holy cities.

TOM. I do not forget that, sir. But your father attacked Medina and failed.

FEISAL. Then the honourable thing for his son is to succeed.

TOM. But you will not. You do not have the men. The British will not help, they have recalled too many troops to Europe, those left are dug in on the border with Gaza.

FEISAL. Then what is your counsel, Captain?

TOM. Keep the Turks in Medina and let them despair.

FEISAL. Despair.

TOM. Attack their supply lines.

FEISAL. The Hejaz Railway? Our fighters do attack it.
(*A shrug*.) There is loot.

TOM. But they do not attack with a plan. We must hit some
trains not others, to bottle them up.

FEISAL. Put them in a bottle?

TOM. It's an English saying.

FEISAL (*English, Arabic accent*). 'Bottle them up.' A
dishonourable idea.

TOM. But effective. Create chaos, be a silent threat, never let
the enemy know when we will come out of the desert to kill,
then disappear.

FEISAL. That is how we have always fought. Another English
saying: 'hit and run'? But I am trying to build an army,
Lawrence. And we need a battle, a true victory. Not just
guerrilla raids.

TOM. I know a battle you can win. Aqaba.

A silence.

FEISAL. If we had Aqaba, the British could supply my forces
from the sea.

TOM. Yes.

FEISAL. We could push north, toward Baghdad.

TOM. Yes.

FEISAL. And the British could supply their forces in Palestine.

TOM (*a beat*). Your Highness has great insight.

FEISAL. No, I just begin to understand British Imperial thinking.

A pause.

Well, it is a pretty idea.

TOM. Very pretty.

FEISAL. But impossible.

TOM. Most deeds are impossible. Until they are done.

FEISAL. The Turks have heavy guns at Aqaba.

TOM. But they are fixed, pointing out to sea. The guns could not be turned on a force that attacks from the land.

FEISAL. When you say 'land', you mean the Negev desert.

TOM. Yes.

A pause.

FEISAL. How do you know about the guns?

TOM. Because I went into Aqaba and looked.

FEISAL. Alone?

TOM. Yes.

FEISAL. No doubt suitably disguised.

LAWRENCE *smiles.*

It is four hundred miles across the Negev to reach Aqaba.

TOM. Yes.

FEISAL. What is it about the English desire to go into difficult places?

TOM. The desert is not difficult for the Bedouin.

FEISAL. Oh, it is. Every dawn, day and night. Do not be mistaken about desert life. Do not, what is the English word? (*Arabic accent.*) 'Romance.'

TOM. I am corrected.

FEISAL. I doubt that! (*Laughs*.) Does Allenby know of your plan?

TOM. I did explain it to him. He said I was mad.

FEISAL. That is true.

FEISAL *laughs again, then is serious*.

I will give you fifty men.

TOM. Fifty.

FEISAL. I will send my cousin to lead them.

TOM. Sherif Nasir is a great fighter, but fifty…

FEISAL. You have met with the Howeitat tribe. I assume Auda Abu Tayi promised you fighters?

TOM. Your Highness is well informed.

FEISAL. And am I well informed about you?

TOM. I am entirely at your service, Prince. And a friend.

FEISAL *looks at him, unreadable. A difficult moment. He continues as if nothing has happened*.

FEISAL. Auda Abu will recruit more men from the Negev tribes as you go south. If you have gold.

TOM. I have gold.

FEISAL. You do? What, on your person? Now?

LAWRENCE *touches his midriff*. FEISAL *laughs*.

You are a wild man, Lawrence. The Arabs are fortunate to have you as a friend. Call your servant, we will send the King of England a message.

FEISAL *gestures. His* MEN *appear again with the chair as* LAWRENCE *shouts*.

TOM. Thomas, you idiot, now!

THOMAS, *with a clattering of tripod, comes on. The group assembles. He takes a picture*.

The desert scene fades and…

Scene Six

CHARLOTTE*'s sitting room at Shaw's Corner.*

It is February 1923. The garden is now wintry.

PATCH *is taking dictation.*

SHAW *paces. Then stops. He adopts a rhetorical pose and is about to speak. Nothing. He paces again. Stops.*

GBS. Why won't Joan move, why won't she speak? I see her very clearly. She's sitting there, on the flagstones of Rheims Cathedral. She was arguing with the French court, telling them to launch another attack on the English. The scene was going so well! Then she… froze on me.

PATCH. Writer's block?

GBS. Writer's block is for wimps.

PATCH. Maybe it's not she who has nothing to say, maybe it's you.

GBS. Name a playwright who had nothing to say.

PATCH. William Shakespeare?

GBS. Nonsense. The man was a secret Catholic. Everything he wrote was Popish propaganda, that's glaringly obvious. Read the last two lines.

PATCH. Dunois has just said: 'I tell you that your little hour of miracles is over, and that from this time on he who plays the war game best will win – if the luck is on his side.' To which Joan replies: 'Ah! If, if, if, if, if! If ifs and ands were pots there'd be no need of tinkers.'

A moment.

GBS. What an earth is she talking about?

PATCH. You should know, you made her say it.

GBS. That is not how it works.

PATCH. Will you ever learn Spanish?

GBS. What has learning Spanish to do with it?

PATCH. In the last twelve months you have purchased three different 'Teach Yourself Spanish' books. Have you opened one of them?

GBS. What is your point?

PATCH. You're lazy.

GBS. Lazy? *Me?* This month I have already written over a thousand letters to correspondents all round the world! Published three Fabian pamphlets, given six lectures and, may I remind you, I have got five scenes of this damn play out, by sweat and heaving!

PATCH. Well, there you go.

GBS. Go where?

She clams up.

Offstage a doorbell rings.

Patch, you so rarely comment at all on our work together. But since you are now, speak up! Where do I go?

PATCH. Stretching yourself thin. Which is a kind of laziness.

GBS. What, you think I'm superficial?

PATCH. I think you are determined to be cheerful. Relentlessly, even wearingly so. But you are attempting to write a tragedy. The old tomfoolery will not work.

ALLENBY (*off*). I do hope this is not inconvenient.

CHARLOTTE (*off*). He is working, but I'm sure he will want to see you.

PATCH. She also believes in God. Which is giving you no end of trouble.

GBS. I hate to own up, but you are right. It is the most difficult thing to write and put upon a stage: human purity.

Enter CHARLOTTE *and* EDMUND ALLENBY – *Viscount and Field Marshal. He is in civilian clothes but they and his bearing shout 'Army'.* CHARLOTTE *is flustered.*

CHARLOTTE. Bernard, we have a caller…

ALLENBY *extends a hand.*

ALLENBY. Delighted to meet you, Mr Shaw. Allenby.

SHAW *stares at him.*

CHARLOTTE. Field Marshal Allenby, dearest.

GBS. And why not?

A vigorous handshake.

Field Marshal, you are very welcome. Forgive me, I was centuries away. In France in 1431 to be precise. I am writing a play about Joan of Arc.

ALLENBY. Ah yes, The Maid. Was she entirely a figment of French propaganda?

SHAW *does not blink. His Irish brogue a little clearer.*

GBS. That could well be so, since it be true that history is written by the victors. And the French did beat you in the Hundred Years War.

ALLENBY. Beat me?

GBS. The English.

ALLENBY. Ah.

SHAW *smiles.* ALLENBY *smiles.*

GBS. Field Marshal, this is Miss Blanche Patch, my moral compass.

ALLENBY. I'm delighted to meet you, Miss Patch.

PATCH. I merely write down what he says.

ALLENBY (*charm*). And, indeed, I'm sure Mr Shaw has a great deal to say.

PATCH. It comes in bursts.

A moment.

I have to type up. Please excuse me.

ALLENBY. Of course…

GBS. Thank you, Patch. (*Gesturing to a seat.*) Field Marshal, please…

ALLENBY. Thank you…

He sits as PATCH *exits.*

CHARLOTTE. Can I offer you something? We have many kinds of teas and there is carrot cake…

ALLENBY. Perhaps a glass of water.

CHARLOTTE. Of course.

CHARLOTTE *exits as if fleeing.*

GBS. If you have a driver, he is welcome to come in. Perhaps he'll try the carrot cake? Chauffeurs are often adventurers.

ALLENBY. Drove myself actually.

GBS. Was it difficult to find us?

ALLENBY. Got utterly lost.

GBS. Ayot St Lawrence is rather tucked away. Writers always dream of rural obscurity.

ALLENBY. Not so obscure. Presumably the fellows hanging around your gate are journalists?

GBS. One is to the press as a jampot is to flies.

ALLENBY. I too have experienced the jampot effect.

GBS. Did they spot who you are?

ALLENBY. I may have got away with it, wearing civvies.

GBS. Ah. (*A moment.*) You're here about Tom Lawrence.

ALLENBY. Yes.

GBS. I'm afraid your expedition into the maze of our
Hertfordshire lanes is pointless, Field Marshal. Mrs Shaw
and I are not at liberty to tell you where Lawrence is.

ALLENBY. Oh, I know where he is. He's at the RAF depot in
Uxbridge, enlisted for basic training as an Aircraftsman
Second Class.

GBS. You know.

ALLENBY. Just about the whole of the War Office knows,
Downing Street knows, the Air Chief Marshal knows.
Lawrence writes to the Marshal every week, complaining
about conditions for the men in the barracks. Even the Palace
knows where the silly bugger is!

CHARLOTTE, *who has heard this, enters carrying a glass
of water.*

CHARLOTTE. Your water.

ALLENBY. Thank you.

GBS. Apparently the whole of the British establishment knows
Tom is in the RAF.

CHARLOTTE. Playing silly buggers.

ALLENBY. I apologise for my language. But absolutely: he is
playing the fool.

CHARLOTTE. Though there is something wonderful about it.

ALLENBY. I see no wonder at all.

GBS. An Army war hero seeks to serve his country with a new
career in the Royal Air Force? Cue trumpets and patriotic
rejoicing. Where is the problem?

ALLENBY. I suspect you are feigning naivety.

GBS. Yes, it's a rhetorical trick. Socrates was always using it,
deeply irritating. But surely Lawrence is free to do what he
likes with his life?

ALLENBY. That is the point. He is not.

GBS. He is not free to join the RAF?

ALLENBY. Under his own name, yes.

GBS. But if he joined the ranks as Lawrence, imagine the ribbing from his fellow recruits! Barrack-room life would be impossible.

ALLENBY. It's offensive, slumming it in the lower ranks.

CHARLOTTE. Oh. Is this all about class?

ALLENBY. Of course it's about class! By enlisting under a false name as a common Aircraftsman, what is the man saying?

CHARLOTTE. 'I am inventing myself anew'?

ALLENBY. Bohemian poppycock.

CHARLOTTE. You should read Nietzsche.

ALLENBY. No thank you. Lawrence is insulting the Army he fought for.

CHARLOTTE. Valiantly…

ALLENBY. Yes, he was a great soldier, and that makes it even worse! He's Lawrence of Arabia, for Godsake! If this gets out it'll be a scandal.

GBS. Why?

ALLENBY. Because you can't have an officer and a gentlemen cleaning lavatories!

GBS. Yes, that does challenge the great, toppling pyramid of the English class system.

ALLENBY. You know he turned down a knighthood.

SHAW *and* CHARLOTTE *look at each other.*

CHARLOTTE. No. We didn't know that.

ALLENBY. He went to the Palace and told the King, face to face. Turned in his DSO medal, too.

CHARLOTTE. What reason did he give?

ALLENBY. It's all been hushed up.

GBS. Why do you think he did it?

ALLENBY. Because he's an unstable little prick!

CHARLOTTE. I will take an apology for that.

ALLENBY. I am not inclined to give it.

A silence.

Oh, damn it, I love the man.

CHARLOTTE. So he really was great in the desert.

ALLENBY. Oh, yes. More than he is ever going to be given credit for.

CHARLOTTE. Aqaba.

ALLENBY. A brilliant operation. You know, at Aqaba, he nearly died?

CHARLOTTE. No, he… No, I didn't know that.

ALLENBY. He accidentally shot his camel in the head.

CHARLOTTE. Oh!

ALLENBY. The beast nearly crushed him.

GBS. That is…

ALLENBY. Farcical? Yes. Farce and death go hand in hand in combat.

GBS. What do you want from us, Field Marshal?

A pause.

ALLENBY. There is a journalist called Lowell Thomas.

CHARLOTTE. Yes…?

ALLENBY. A very insistent chap. Yesterday finally badgered his way into my club. He claims that you are in contact with Lawrence.

SHAW *sighs.*

Please understand. He has been to the recruiting office in Charlotte Street where Lawrence enlisted. Journalists seem to have a ratlike ability to go through small holes. And, I fear, he is driven by some kind of personal grudge. At any moment Uxbridge could be all over the newspapers, there'll be a national outcry and Lawrence will be hounded.

GBS. So you want us to persuade Tom to take a commission in the RAF under his own name?

ALLENBY. You are his friends. You can tell him to stop his nonsense.

GBS. Well, fat chance of that. Even if we wished to, which we do not.

A silence.

ALLENBY. I am trying to rescue him from himself.

GBS. So are we.

ALLENBY. But you are… artistic people.

CHARLOTTE. Oh dear, does it show?

SHAW *laughs,* ALLENBY *is not amused.*

ALLENBY. And coming from your milieu, I fear you do not realise the seriousness of what Lawrence has done. It would have been better for him to have been shot in the desert.

GBS. Better be with the worms in the grave than be seen slumming with the working class?

ALLENBY. For an officer and war hero of his standing, yes! The pity of it is he has so much to offer, the man's a natural leader, he could do wonderful things, be a statesman, anything… But the English state does not forgive. If he continues to behave like this, all that potential will pass for nothing, doors will be slammed in his face, he'll be destroyed.

GBS. If Tom Lawrence wants to burn alive, his friends must respect his choice.

A pause.

ALLENBY. So, nothing to be done?

GBS. No.

ALLENBY. This will be a tragedy for him.

CHARLOTTE. Or his salvation.

ALLENBY. Well. That will be as it will be.

>ALLENBY *stands*.

I have enjoyed your plays, Mr Shaw. I thought *Arms and the Man* was very funny.

GBS. The King said the author must be mad.

ALLENBY. A soldier with chocolates in his gun holster? Absolutely believable. (*Hesitates for a moment*.) Whatever happens, take care of Lawrence. He's one in a million. And many people don't like that.

GBS. Let me see you to your car.

ALLENBY. Thank you. Mrs Shaw.

>*Going*.

CHARLOTTE. Field Marshal, what happened to Lawrence at Daraa?

>*A silence*.

ALLENBY. How do you know about Lawrence in Daraa?

CHARLOTTE. I am helping him edit his book about the Desert War.

ALLENBY. Oh yes, 'the book'.

CHARLOTTE. It's that I can't quite understand what happened.

ALLENBY. I had an account from a friend of Lawrence, Frank Stirling.

CHGARLOTTE. Yes, I have some of their letters…

ALLENBY. He went into the town on reconnaissance. He was in disguise. It was a damn fool thing to do. The Turks captured him, there was some beastliness and Lawrence got beaten up. But he managed to get away.

CHARLOTTE. And that is it?

ALLENBY. Yes.

CHARLOTTE. That is all that happened?

ALLENBY. Mrs Shaw, in war a fog can fall. It can make the stories of war… obscure. Do not bother with Daraa.

CHARLOTTE. Do not bother my woman's head, you mean?

ALLENBY. I'm not saying anything about a woman's head or some such… But if you are editing the damn book, you would be advised to cut any mention of Daraa.

CHARLOTTE. Why? I will not let this go.

He stares at her, then…

ALLENBY. The trouble with Lawrence, brilliant though he be, is that at heart he is one of you.

CHARLOTTE. One of us?

ALLENBY. An artist. And arts in war are a pain in the backside. Good day.

SHAW *grimaces at* CHARLOTTE *as he and* ALLENBY *exit.*

CHARLOTTE *paces. She goes to the manuscript, opens it, reads, closes it in distress. Pages fall on the floor.*

CHARLOTTE. Oh foodle di, foodle foo.

She stoops to pick them up.

As she is doing so SHAW *enters.*

GBS. Oh my dear…

CHARLOTTE. I just…

GBS. It's all right…

She is still crouched.

CHARLOTTE. I'm so afraid for Tom.

GBS. Charlotte, please…

He helps her to a chair. She composes herself.

CHARLOTTE. We can't let him burn.

GBS. Public opinion is a deadly fire.

CHARLOTTE. Is that really how you see him? The innocent holy warrior, at the stake?

GBS. It's the writer's vice: looking at the world through the lens of your latest work.

CHARLOTTE. Bernard, seriously, we must do everything we can.

GBS. Absolutely. We will help our man of many wiles.

CHARLOTTE. Poor Tom: a mixture of Odysseus and St Joan? No wonder he's going potty.

GBS. Or seriously sane.

They look at each other. Then they burst into laughter.

CHARLOTTE. What would Allenby have done if he'd known he is in a room just up there?

GBS. Rushed up the stairs and challenged him to pistols on our lawn!

CHARLOTTE. I was terrified he was going to come down. I feel naughty.

GBS. It's like a house-party game: hide the hero.

CHARLOTTE. But it's not a game at all, really.

GBS. No.

CHARLOTTE. If Lowell Thomas does expose him, what are we going to do?

GBS. I haven't the faintest idea.

Enter LAWRENCE. *He is in RAF uniform. He is cheerful.*

TOM. Has the big beast gone?

They stare a him. Then...

GBS. He has ridden off in his Daimler, scattering Fleet Street's finest.

TOM. He's a great man, you know, you mustn't think badly of him.

GBS. Oh, I think *very* badly of him. His record fighting against the Boers was appalling.

TOM. Did you bring that up?

GBS. I exercised superhuman self-restraint.

TOM. In order to come here, he would have done the same. He thinks you are an Irish Fenian.

GBS. I am. And he is a British Imperialist.

TOM. You know that when Allenby entered Jerusalem, at the head of his British and Arab forces, he went on foot, out of respect? And then declared the city open to all faiths. He's a sensitive man.

GBS. Imperial sensitivity. Yes, we've had a lot of that in Ireland.

CHARLOTTE. Bernard...

TOM. Let's just say we are each a little self-contained army, clashing with others in the night.

GBS. Yes, Arnold, 'ignorant armies that clash by night', I detest that line.

CHARLOTTE. Bernard, *please* don't fly off...

BERNARD. I will fly off, bit between the teeth, no going back. (*To* LAWRENCE.) I had a drunkard father. They all said he didn't know what he was doing. But of course he did! We all know very well what we're doing, the problem is to make ourselves own up! As I think you should. Tom, what are you doing?

A pause.

CHARLOTTE. Yes, Tom, so many things, what… (*Doesn't go there*.) Why did you turn down a knighthood?

TOM. Allenby told you about that?

CHARLOTTE. Yes, but not why.

TOM. I went to see His Majesty privately. I did it discreetly, I didn't want a public fuss. (*A beat*.) And I returned my Distinguished Service Medal which I won because of Aqaba.

GBS. What was the look on the King's…

CHARLOTTE. Shut up, Bernard.

A pause.

TOM. I did so in protest at the British Government's policies towards the Arabs. They helped us win the war against the Ottoman Empire. Without that help, we would have lost the Middle East. (*A beat*.) And they helped us win because we promised them that, after the war, there would be one great nation, independent, and free, with Damascus as its capital. (*A beat*.) But we have gone back on our word. We have divided their lands and occupied them. The British in Iraq, the French in Syria, the British in Palestine… Iraq, Syria, Palestine… before these were areas, like songs in the heart, not carved-up countries with straight lines, drawn with rulers on maps by bureaucrats in distant offices in Paris and London, straight through tribal lands. There are no countries, only… the Arabs! A nation that roams across the deserts, the wadis and the oases, that trades along coasts all the way to Africa and India… A nation without borders, complex, tribal, with rival traditions held in a delicate balance, united by two things – a language and a Holy Book. (*A beat*.) We are in bad faith. And it will not be forgiven. Because of our straight lines we will bring chaos and reap a whirlwind. (*A beat*.) So I chucked the medal and said no to the royal breadknife, because I am ashamed of my country.

A pause.

GBS. My dear fellow, you are the most imperious, anti-imperialist I have ever met.

SHAW *shakes his hand.*

CHARLOTTE. And… (*Goes there.*) what happened in Daraa?

LAWRENCE *stares at her.*

All three very still.

Enter PATCH, *quickly, with a copy of* The Times *open.*

PATCH. Look. 'Colonel Lawrence Enlisted in RAF Under False Name'.

CHARLOTTE. Oh, please not…

CHARLOTTE *hastily takes the newspaper from her and reads.*

GBS. Patch, tell Higgs and his garden boy to stand by the gates with suitably sharp gardening implements. We do not want an incursion by the fourth estate.

PATCH *exits quickly.*

CHARLOTTE. Uxbridge depot… John Hume Ross… Aircraftsman second class… They know everything. It must be Lowell Thomas.

LAWRENCE *smiles, then begins to laugh. His laughter grows. They stare at him, not joining in.* LAWRENCE *wipes his eyes.*

TOM. Isn't it wonderful being alive!

End of Act One.

ACT TWO

Scene One

A few days later.

Shaw's Corner, CHARLOTTE*'s sitting room.*

THOMAS *and* CHARLOTTE *are standing still, staring at each other.*

A pause.

CHARLOTTE. Very well. I'll try.

THOMAS. That is very good of you.

> *She turns and exits. And enters at once. She goes quickly to a table and picks up a bulky manuscript.*

'Fraid I'd steal something, Mrs Shaw?

CHARLOTTE. Absolutely.

> *She hesitates, then...*

My husband is at present in a tea room on Crewe railway station. It is also the servants' day off, so I am in charge of the house. I hope there will be no unpleasantness, Mr Thomas.

THOMAS. I'm saddened you think so low of me, Mrs Shaw.

CHARLOTTE. Well, I do.

> *She exits quickly, clutching the manuscript.*

> THOMAS *makes a 'tsk' noise, sighs and looks around the room. Photographs on a table attract his attention. He peers at them.*

> LAWRENCE *enters, wearing the robes.*

THOMAS. My God. Full regalia.

TOM. You wanted Lawrence of Arabia? Well, here he is, one last time. Among friends.

THOMAS. Friends? Really? Seen these photographs? (*Points to one after the other.*) Lenin. Dzerzhinsky. Ibsen. Dzerzhinsky, for crying out loud! Head of the Soviet Union secret police! (*Points again.*) A terrorist, a torturer and a pornographic playwright. These are the heroes of your friends?

TOM. There are worlds within worlds.

THOMAS. They're bohemians and damn near communistic with it. Why are you slumming it with these degenerates?

TOM. If you are going to insult the Shaws, this interview is over.

THOMAS. Oh! Is that why you think I'm here? To get a goddamn interview?

TOM. Well, isn't it? Am I not, at the moment, what is the phrase, 'hot press'? A 'scoop'?

THOMAS. Okay okay okay. Let's calm down, both of us are angry.

TOM. What have you got to be angry about?

THOMAS. The way you have treated me.

TOM. The way *I* have treated *you*?

THOMAS. You've got to get on board with me, Tom. You've got no choice.

TOM. Is that a threat?

THOMAS. No choice because… In God's name, man, you're Lawrence of Arabia! The public won't let you be anything else, no one will let you be anything else. They want their hero back.

TOM. What, as a freak show? Waving these… (*Flicks the robes.*) around on the back of a wooden camel, on tour, the Albert Hall to village huts?

THOMAS. And Carnegie Hall in New York and venues in thirty states… don't sniff at it, fella: a place in history. I'll give you the bottom line, Tom. You deserve great fame, but this is the modern world and you've got to work for it.

TOM. 'Work for fame'? That is… ob…

He collects himself.

You saw what I did in the desert. You saw how Prince Feisal's fighters lived with death. You took great photographs that meant something… but hunting me down like this? To degrade me as a fairground spectacle? The Arabs would call that 'dishonourable'. And you know what they do to people who question their honour. Involves neck and sword.

THOMAS. Going to chop my head off and send it rolling across an English lawn, Tom?

TOM. The image does appeal.

A pause.

THOMAS. You used me to make yourself famous.

TOM. You used me to make money!

THOMAS. Yes, the lectures make a buck. I'm not ashamed of that. I don't live on ambrosia on your mountaintop for heroes, I have to grub about down below to make a living. And you said the lectures help the Arab cause.

TOM. The Arab cause is lost. What's the point of going on about someone called Lawrence of Arabia, when everything he believed in failed?

THOMAS. You don't get it, do you, you really don't. You're loved, you're England's darling hero.

TOM. Not now you've told England its hero ran away to slum it in the RAF with the smelly lower orders.

THOMAS. That wasn't me! That was your goddamn gutter press, I can put it to rights.

TOM. I think not, the public have glimpsed the reality behind your 'King of the Desert'.

THOMAS. 'Reality'? (*Laughs*.) Reality's just stuff, like dough, pummel it into any shape you want, then shove it in the great oven of publicity. God, Tom! What is it you want?

TOM. I want the lower depths. An animal level below which a man cannot fall. That's what I want.

A pause.

THOMAS. You know, I've never really known what to make of you. But I do now. You disgust me.

TOM. Good. Because I disgust myself.

A pause.

THOMAS. So... I take it you're not going to honour the contract you had with me?

A faint smile from LAWRENCE.

So be it. (*Turns to go but then turns back*.) I have built my life round you. Dear God, my life is all about you. And what are you? A goddamn little queer.

THOMAS *exits*.

LAWRENCE *alone*.

TOM. What am I?

The garden dissolving...

I... I... I...

He stumbles away, falls in sand. His robes are dirtied. He struggles to his feet.

And...

Scene Two

9 July 1917. Cairo. ALLENBY*'s office.*

Enter ALLENBY.

TOM. Good morning, sir.

ALLENBY. Good God, man, what are you wearing?

TOM. Arab robes, sir.

ALLENBY. Why?

TOM. They're convenient. Airy in the heat. And they can save on underwear.

ALLENBY *glares, then laughs.*

ALLENBY. What a rum fellow you are, Lawrence. So where the hell have you come from, in skirts and stinking like a walking armpit?

TOM. From Aqaba, sir. We've taken the town.

A beat.

ALLENBY. Aqaba has fallen? Despite the guns?

TOM. The guns were fixed, pointing to the sea.

ALLENBY. We were not sure of that.

TOM. I was. I disguised myself as an Arab and went on a reconnaissance of the town. I can pass myself off as a Circassian. They're fair-skinned and I know the dialect.

ALLENBY. And so you…

TOM. Attacked from the land.

ALLENBY. Out of the Negev. One of the most inhospitable places on earth, an incredible feat, Lawrence.

TOM. Thank you, sir. Though there are tribes living there. They think it's… just the world.

Grins.

ALLENBY. Intolerable for us, though. How long did it take you to cross?

TOM. Eight weeks. We had to zigzag, riding hard from well to well. We created diversions to fool the Turks about the direction we were going in, blew up a few things along the way of course. (*Grins*.) Actually the big fight was before we got to the town. An outpost at a place called Aba el Lissan. The Turks had dug in, took us all day to winkle them out. Then the town was more or less open to us.

ALLENBY. 'Us'?

TOM. Arab forces. Prince Feisal gave the operation his blessing.

ALLENBY. And Aqaba is in their hands.

TOM. They're waiting for British reinforcements to come by sea, to set up a garrison.

ALLENBY. Which will be done at once. Derring-do, eh? Like a boy's adventure book!

TOM (*disapproving*). Hardly that, sir.

ALLENBY. Speaks a man who's just crossed the Sinai to report.

TOM. That was nothing, a forty-eight-hour ride. My camel could smell the water of the Nile, a hundred miles away. (*Grins*.)

ALLENBY. I think… (*A beat.*) I think I owe you an apology.

TOM. Not at all, sir…

ALLENBY. Shut up, I'm being gracious.

TOM. Yes, sir.

ALLENBY. Which is a bloody difficult thing to do with you, Lawrence. You really are… Well… Yes.

TOM. Sir?

ALLENBY. I mean, when you talked of raising an Arab force to attack Aqaba, my staff said you were potty. They thought: Let him go and get himself killed in the sand.

TOM. You did give me twenty thousand pounds in gold, sir.

ALLENBY. And sweated somewhat when you disappeared into the desert with it. So, the revolt is real?

TOM. Yes.

ALLENBY. Convince me. What about their communications, intelligence of the enemy?

TOM. The Bedouin have an uncanny sense of where everyone is, at any time. I don't know how they do it. But they knew you visited the front in Gaza, two weeks ago.

ALLENBY. So much for 'a highly secret inspection'…

TOM. And their intelligence is priceless. Many of them have deserted from the Turkish Army. They know their enemies by name.

ALLENBY. You idolise them, don't you.

TOM. They can be tricky sods.

ALLENBY. Do their troops obey orders?

TOM. They're not troops, they're fighters. And they obey their hearts.

ALLENBY. That sounds highly unreliable.

TOM. Not at all. It's in their hearts to kill Turks.

ALLENBY. Mm. (*A pause.*) All right. Let them say I'm mad, but I'm going along with this. I'm bumping you up to Colonel.

TOM. I'm honoured, sir.

ALLENBY. I'll make it a field promotion. Never given one of 'em before, rather fun. Terrific show, Lawrence. Now, go to the mess, get some sleep, freshen up, my valet will send over a uniform and we'll have a bloody good dinner tonight with my staff.

TOM. Thank you, sir.

ALLENBY *thinks that is that, but* LAWRENCE *does not move.*

ALLENBY. Something else, Lawrence?

TOM. Yes, sir. I've promised the Arabs their freedom.

A silence.

ALLENBY. I'm sorry, what did you say?

TOM. I've promised the Arabs their freedom.

A beat.

ALLENBY. So?

TOM. So… that's what they must have.

ALLENBY. Look, of course you say things over the campfires. Give out encouragement, keep things together.

TOM. I have made a solemn promise to Prince Feisal. If he continues to fight the Turks under British command, after the war we will make him the head of a government of all the Arabs. With Damascus as its capital.

ALLENBY. You're a British Army Officer! You have no business making promises to…

Stops himself.

TOM. To a bunch of towel-heads?

ALLENBY. Don't put words in my mouth! I have always made a point of respecting other cultures.

TOM. But not up to the point of giving them freedom?

ALLENBY. Absolutely not!

TOM (*lower*). They may just take it, of course.

ALLENBY. Lawrence, is Arab stuff leaking into you?

TOM. Leaking, sir?

ALLENBY. Be careful. I've seen some very tough nuts lose their way: finding mystery in sand dunes, going all out for hashish pipes, Sufi stories, Arab slippers… (*A gesture.*) robes.

TOM. I'm being practical, sir. I want the Arabs to fight with us, against the Turks.

ALLENBY. And you can rely on them to fight?

TOM. Utterly. To death. But…

ALLENBY. But they won't if they think the British will stay in the region, after the war.

TOM. No.

ALLENBY. I begin to see it. A promise of freedom makes military sense.

LAWRENCE *is being very careful.*

TOM. That's what I'm trying to say, sir.

ALLENBY. Very well. Promise them the earth if that keeps them fighting.

TOM. But I must believe what I promise them.

ALLENBY. Of course. Colonel Lawrence, you are a British Intelligence Officer. When you're out there in some godforsaken desert hole, with sand up your Arab skirt around your testicles, remember that your loyalty is to the British Crown.

TOM. And so… the Arabs will take Damascus.

ALLENBY. Yes.

The scene dissolving.

TOM. Damascus.

He stumbles away, half-falls in the sand, dirtying his robes further. And exits.

Scene Three

Damascus. 1 October 1918.

Off: celebratory small-arms fire, shouting.

Enter FEISAL *with* FIGHTERS. *They are heavily armed and laughing.*

Enter LAWRENCE – *in robes. He has a rifle across his shoulder and a band of ammunition.*

They stop celebrating and stare at him.

TOM. I have just come from the Turkish barracks! What I saw there is a disgrace!

    FEISAL *turns to the* FIGHTERS *who exit.*

    To be in Damascus and do that!

FEISAL. They were Turks.

TOM. A room full of corpses.

FEISAL. Turkish corpses.

TOM. They had surrendered!

FEISAL. The years of Turkish oppression have to be avenged.

TOM. Your fighters are out of control.

FEISAL. Theirs is the prize.

TOM. They will loot the whole city.

FEISAL. A few things will be taken. Furniture! We are a nomadic people but we love furniture. It is wholly impractical to our way of life, but I have seen wardrobes, Western-style dressing tables with mirrors, swaying into the sunset on the backs of camels. (*Laughs.*) We are in Damascus, Lawrence, be happy.

TOM. With the greatest respect, Your Highness. You have no idea of the danger you face. If they see this chaos, the British will take over the city.

FEISAL. You mean you will fight us?

TOM. Me? I would never fight you.

FEISAL. But you are a British Army Officer.

TOM. And I am your adviser!

FEISAL. Yes.

TOM. And your comrade-in-arms.

FEISAL. You have been. (*A beat*.) But if you were ordered by Allenby to fire on a pack of looting, rabid-dog Arabs, you will disobey orders?

LAWRENCE *is shocked*.

TOM. Your Highness, how do I deserve to be…

FEISAL. You think you are deserving?

A beat.

TOM. Prove to the British and the allies that you can rule. Establish order. Make Arab authority a political reality that cannot be denied. You have two, maybe three more days to do it.

FEISAL. So, yet again, I have to impress. Forever a child who has to prove he is a man?

TOM. I have to tell you a secret.

FEISAL. Oh, you have a secret, do you, Lawrence.

TOM. There is a man called Sir Mark Sykes. A British Member of Parliament. I met him in Hejaz three weeks ago. He told me… He boasted to me… that an agreement will be announced. Any day now. It's a treaty between the British and the French, signed nearly three years ago, before the Revolt even began! In the eyes of God, I swear I knew nothing of it. Sykes and a Frenchman have drawn a line in the sand from the Mediterranean to the Persian border. They have conjured countries out of thin air. The British get Iraq with Baghdad as its capital, and Palestine. The French get

Syria. Sir, in these days, you have the chance. The one chance. To show yourself worthy of ruling your people.

A silence.

FEISAL. Sir Mark Sykes visited my father in Medina.

A silence.

TOM. He visited Prince Hussein…

FEISAL. You are all Imperialist dogs. I led a revolt against the Turks, now I will lead a revolt against the French and the British. I am going to declare myself King of Syria.

LAWRENCE *is shocked.*

TOM. I beg you, do not do that. The French will move against you at once.

FEISAL. Then where is the freedom for the Arab peoples, Lawrence?

A pause.

TOM. Your Highness, I'll talk to the British Government.

FEISAL. I will be King of Syria.

TOM. Sir, you will be…

FEISAL. What? Shot? Imprisoned? Exiled? (*Smiles.*) We will see.

TOM. I will go to London. Immediately. I will speak for you.

FEISAL. You speak for me?

TOM. I have, throughout the war.

FEISAL. No.

A beat.

TOM. I beg you, my prince, you don't understand the situation…

FEISAL. Don't I? Colonel Lawrence?

A silence.

I always knew you lied to me.

TOM. I am deeply saddened to hear Your Highness say so.

FEISAL. Truth is a bitter herb.

They look at each other.

TOM. We have fought together.

FEISAL. We have.

TOM. Heat and cold, so many nights.

FEISAL. So many.

TOM. And days of thirst and hunger and of triumph and
feasting.

FEISAL. They remain in my memory.

TOM. And in mine.

A pause, both dead still.

FEISAL. But you have always had only one master. British
Intelligence in Cairo, run by General Allenby.

TOM. I have pleaded with him, I have pleaded with men above
him, to make the case for Arabia...

FEISAL. No. You lied to us to make us fight. For the British
Empire.

TOM. I believe in your cause.

FEISAL. King George of England is your prince, not I. Go now.

They stare at each other.

Then FEISAL exits.

LAWRENCE *alone. He exits.*

Scene Four

CHARLOTTE*'s sitting room.*

CHARLOTTE *and* PATCH. *They are both working on manuscript pages.*

On a small table there is a tea set and a small cake stand, loaded.

PATCH. So. We've almost finished spying in the Syrian towns.

CHARLOTTE. Yes, we've done splendidly.

PATCH. I didn't realise that it rained so much in the winter.

CHARLOTTE. So harsh. But the way Tom describes it, the desert is so beautiful, even in the wet and cold.

PATCH. Yes. (*A beat.*) Colonel Lawrence is very trusting.

CHARLOTTE. Trusting?

Enter SHAW.

GBS. Mrs Higgs tells me that that fellow Thomas called this morning. And she and Mr Higgs were out.

CHARLOTTE. Don't worry. We have counted the spoons.

GBS. Was he unpleasant?

CHARLOTTE. Highly.

GBS. Did Tom agree to see him?

CHARLOTTE. Yes.

A pause.

GBS. Well? Was there an altercation? Lovely word, you can hear knuckles cracking in the syllables.

CHARLOTTE. I don't know what was said.

GBS. No Hamlet-like sneaking about behind the arras?

CHARLOTTE. I do not sneak.

GBS. Of course not. But imagine standing behind one of Morris's heavy curtains, to hear the great and good confessing all in our own sitting room.

CHARLOTTE. *My* sitting room.

GBS. Yes, of course. Free in our own spaces, the way to live.

A pause.

CHARLOTTE. Bernard, I am busy.

GBS. The mighty editing. Onward!

He makes to go but does not.

Where's Tom now?

CHARLOTTE. Upstairs, resting.

GBS. Mood?

CHARLOTTE. Can you read Tom's mood? Can you read anyone's?

GBS. Ah.

PATCH *making to stand.*

PATCH. Perhaps I will…

CHARLOTTE. You stay where you are, Patch, we haven't finished.

GBS. Frost at midnight.

CHARLOTTE. Or at five o'clock in the afternoon.

A pause.

GBS. Well, I finished the trial scene!

CHARLOTTE. Bully for you.

GBS. I knew you'd be pleased. I have it in shorthand. I would like Patch to type it up.

CHARLOTTE. Blanche is helping me at the moment. As I said, we are busy.

A beat, both looking at each other.

GBS. Did the quince jelly set?

CHARLOTTE. Yes.

GBS. You tested it on a plate? It congealed in wrinkles?

CHARLOTTE. Yes! Yes! The quince jelly wrinkled!

GBS. I am greatly concerned for him. I fear he may do something rash. I don't want this house to witness something like that.

CHARLOTTE. Then, my dear… Speak to him.

GBS. I don't think I know how to. (*A beat.*) Quince jelly!

He exits.

CHARLOTTE. He dreads tragedy.

PATCH. I know.

CHARLOTTE. Why did you say Tom is trusting?

PATCH. He's given you all his papers. (*A beat.*) His diaries, too.

CHARLOTTE. I've been corresponding with the British Museum Library. When we've finished *Seven Pillars*, and the shortened version, they will be very pleased to take it all.

PATCH. He's just casting things aside?

CHARLOTTE. Like a snake, shedding his skin for a new one. He's extraordinary, isn't he.

PATCH. A snake.

A beat.

CHARLOTTE. Blanche, what?

PATCH. It… no.

CHARLOTTE. What?

PATCH *shakes her head.*

What?

PATCH. I have no opinions.

CHARLOTTE. Blanche Patch, you have so many repressed
opinions that sometimes I wonder you don't explode.

PATCH. It… Why does Colonel Lawrence want us to edit out
what happened in Daraa?

CHARLOTTE. That's all in the *Seven Pillars*, we're cutting out
the purple passages. We're editing things down for a
shortened version.

PATCH. But isn't it all 'good stuff'? Isn't that what the Colonel
wants? Captured by the Turks, tortured by them, only to
escape? Since the edited book is for the wider reader, I
would have thought their eyes would be very wide indeed.

CHARLOTTE. You think it's all derring-do.

PATCH. I think it's the kind of thing Englishmen get up to in
the desert.

CHARLOTTE. You disapprove of Colonel Lawrence.

PATCH. He's… shadowy.

CHARLOTTE. To me he's radiant!

PATCH, *stony*.

Why 'shadowy'?

PATCH. There's a darkness.

CHARLOTTE. He's fought in a war.

PATCH. It's something else.

CHARLOTTE. You're saying this because of what happened to
him in Daraa?

PATCH. I say nothing. I know you admire him.

CHARLOTTE. I do. Greatly.

PATCH, *buttoned up*.

A pause.

Please give me an opinion on my admiration for Colonel
Lawrence.

PATCH. I wouldn't dare.

CHARLOTTE. Oh yes you will! You've started to say something here and I will get to the bottom of it.

PATCH. Daraa.

A pause. PATCH *waits.*

CHARLOTTE. Yes?

PATCH. A Syrian town, garrisoned by the Turks. And a rail hub.

CHARLOTTE. Yes.

PATCH. Despatching troops to a wide area. Despite Lawrence and his fighters blowing up rail tracks.

CHARLOTTE. Yes.

PATCH. The town is well defended. No obvious way of getting a force into the town.

CHARLOTTE. No.

PATCH. So Lawrence decides to go into the town, with a single companion, to spy out the defences.

CHARLOTTE. What is your point?

PATCH. Lawrence is spotted. Arrested.

CHARLOTTE. The Turks don't realise he is British, he passes himself off as Circassian, he can speak the dialect, yes, he did the same to get into Aqaba... The point, Patch?

PATCH. He's accused of being a deserter. He denies it. He's told he's now a recruit in the Turkish Army. He's bathed. He's taken to a house on the outskirts of the town, and up into a bedroom. The Governor of the town is there. Hajim Bey. He orders Lawrence to be stripped.

CHARLOTTE. We've read the horror of it, don't let's dwell...

PATCH. Bey hints that he knows who Lawrence is. Actually, there's a letter, in the letters box file, from Frank Stirling, Lawrence had written to him telling him about the rape.

CHARLOTTE. Attempted rape, Lawrence struggled…

PATCH. Did he?

A beat.

CHARLOTTE. What are you saying?

PATCH. Lawrence's letter to Stirling tells a different story…

CHARLOTTE. But he told Stirling he fought off the Bey's advances.

PATCH. And was taken away and beaten. Horribly.

CHARLOTTE. Yes.

PATCH. With a Circassian whip. Blow after blow, welt on welt. Open wounds, cut again and again.

CHARLOTTE. You're revelling in it.

PATCH. He did.

A pause.

CHARLOTTE. I've wondered about it too. Wondered what really happened. I'm afraid it was far worse.

PATCH. It was.

CHARLOTTE *chooses not to hear that.*

CHARLOTTE. But he escaped! Thrown into a shed, left to bleed, but someone left the door open. I think that was a kindness, don't you? Even in that terrible place, someone who was kind.

A pause. CHARLOTTE *is very uneasy.*

Why do you say it was far worse?

PATCH. Because it didn't happen.

A pause.

CHARLOTTE. What do you mean?

PATCH. He made it up.

PATCH *reaches for a small notebook and opens it.*

This… is his pocket diary. The pages for November 15th to the 21st, when he said he was in Daraa…

Holds the diary out.

CHARLOTTE. They're…

PATCH. Torn out.

CHARLOTTE. But that doesn't…

PATCH. There's a letter to his mother…

Shuffles through papers.

…here… he copied it. Sent on the 14th of November. He says he is going to stay at the castle in Asraq for a few days. Nothing about Daraa.

CHARLOTTE. But look here, on the page for November 14th, it says 'To Harun'. Harun's an area close to Daraa, isn't it?

PATCH. But look at the writing. The hand and the ink. It's different. He added it much later.

CHARLOTTE. Maybe… maybe he tore the pages out in disgust.

PATCH. Or tore them out because he was giving the diary to you.

CHARLOTTE. To deceive me?

PATCH. People who knew him in the war are falling over to publish their accounts. None of them mentions Daraa. And Lawrence was in Aqaba a week later, after a hard ride, apparently in the best of health. No sign of terrible injuries.

CHARLOTTE. What a terrier with a bone you are, Patch.

PATCH. Truth is truth. Before the *Seven Pillars* is published, you'll have to get him to cut it.

CHARLOTTE. How do I possibly accuse him of lying?

PATCH. You… accuse him of lying.

The room has darkened.

Enter SHAW *with a big glowing oil lamp.*

GBS. Can we do the trial scene now, Patch?

PATCH (*looking at* CHARLOTTE). Yes, I think I've helped enough here.

GBS. Ideas are fizzing, I fear I may pop. If we go down to the hut and I dictate, can you use the typewriter there?

PATCH. Of course.

CHARLOTTE. It's cold.

GBS. Bracing! We'll bundle up. I knocked on Tom's door. No reply. If he emerges, send down the garden for me?

CHARLOTTE. Yes.

GBS. Right, Patch, my big scene! The triumph of English might over innocence. Proved hollow, of course.

PATCH (*looking at* CHARLOTTE). Of course.

GBS. The quince jelly looks a lovely colour.

SHAW *and* PATCH *exit.*

CHARLOTTE *alone. She sits still for a while.*

Then she stands and goes around the lamps, turning them on.

She sits at the table again, looking at the mess of papers. She picks up the diary, opens and looks at it. Then she quickly pushes it beneath the table to hide it.

She holds her head in her hands.

She straightens, smooths her dress. She stands and...

LAWRENCE *enters. He is dressed in civilian clothes. There is something of the awkward, conventional military man about him – an echo of the clothes* ALLENBY *was wearing.*

TOM. Charlotte...

CHARLOTTE. Tom.

TOM. I'm so sorry to drag my ill fame into your house.

CHARLOTTE. Don't be silly.

TOM. I know you and Bernard do all you can here to keep the mad world away.

CHARLOTTE. Tom, it is all right.

TOM. You are so kind to give me shelter.

CHARLOTTE laughs.

What?

CHARLOTTE. No.

TOM. What?

CHARLOTTE. It's so strange to see you in ordinary clothes.

TOM. Does it make me look anonymous?

CHARLOTTE. It makes you stand out like a sore thumb. There's still some camomile tea, do you want some? The cake is fennel and dandelion. It's one of Mrs Higgs's more extreme experiments.

TOM. I am all for extreme experiments.

CHARLOTTE. Could you pour? My hands are bad today.

TOM. Of course.

He pours tea, paying careful attention. CHARLOTTE sits, watching him. He cuts portions of cake. They settle.

LAWRENCE has a slice of cake on a small plate. They both look at it.

He lifts the cake and eats it. He chews carefully and swallows.

CHARLOTTE. Well?

TOM. It is… endurable.

They laugh. But for her the laughter dies.

CHARLOTTE. So many things in this house we throw together, always with such enthusiasm, incongruous ingredients, mad

ideas with great hopes... and we are lucky if anything turns
out just about endurable.

TOM. But you've done great things, Charlotte. I'm no socialist,
but you, Bernard and the Webbs, you're changing this
country, and for the better.

CHARLOTTE. Are we? Name an achievement.

TOM. The Fabian Society.

She scoffs.

CHARLOTTE. It's all what we call in Ireland blather and babble.

TOM. Not so, your pamphlets, your campaigns, you keep the
Left in this country democratic. And a really great
achievement: you founded the London School of Economics.

CHARLOTTE. I begin to wonder. It's going very pro-capitalist.
Keynes seems to think markets can actually work.

TOM. What matters is you believe in enlightenment.

CHARLOTTE. Yes.

She looks at him.

But only out of fear of the dark.

*Her hand trembles, with difficulty she replaces her cup in
its saucer.*

TOM. It's worse.

CHARLOTTE. It's in the nature of arthritis to get worse.
Actually... the arthritis is caused by something else.

TOM. Oh, Charlotte, what?

CHARLOTTE. Do the names of our diseases matter?

TOM. If they can be cured...

CHARLOTTE. This can't. It's called Paget's disease. See?
Neither of us is any the wiser.

TOM. What... what do you do about the pain?

CHARLOTTE. What do you?

They are looking at each other, very still.

I look to heal the inner life. I write prayers, asking for peace within. But I don't know to whom, or to what, the prayers are written. Certainly not God.

TOM. I hate the inner life. I want to kill it.

CHARLOTTE. Is that why you hurt yourself? Or get someone else to hurt you?

A pause.

When I first found you sleeping down here, I saw your back. The wounds looked new.

LAWRENCE *takes a breath and is suddenly all energy.*

TOM. Shall we got on with the shorter *Pillars*?

CHARLOTTE *is relieved at the diversion.*

CHARLOTTE. Yes, let's. We've just one or two things to decide…

TOM. I've been thinking of calling it *Revolt in the Desert*.

CHARLOTTE. Right.

TOM. Less poetic than the *Seven Pillars of Wisdom*. And I think I'll leave out the chapter about the Turkish barracks in Damascus.

CHARLOTTE. But that's a wonderful piece of writing.

TOM. And it's a horror.

CHARLOTTE. Isn't that the point?

TOM. I'm trying to make the shorter book calmer, less… purple and poetic. The Damascus scene coming at the end is too bitter, too strong, out of place. Like a sultana in a sponge cake.

CHARLOTTE. Too 'experimental'?

TOM. Yes! A touch too much literary dandelion, I think.

He grins. She turns a paper, disapproving.

CHARLOTTE. Well, it's your work.

TOM. It's a book for the general reader, Charlotte. Forget art. All that matters is to get the story read.

CHARLOTTE. But aren't you doing what Lowell Thomas does with his lectures?

TOM. It's not at all like Thomas's obscene circus. I just want to tell the history of the Arab Revolt plainly.

CHARLOTTE. And truthfully.

TOM. Of course. And I must admit, I'm broke. Good sales would get me out of a hole. (*Grins.*) Not very heroic.

CHARLOTTE. I understand, this is a writer's house.

TOM. Funny thing with heroes. They're not meant to be human. People never imagine them having bank overdrafts.

CHARLOTTE. I've often thought that. Did Hamlet ever go to the lavatory?

They look at each other then laugh.

And what about Daraa?

TOM. Oh, I think all that will go.

A pause.

CHARLOTTE. You'll cut the whole episode.

TOM. Too much purple sprouting broccoli, passed off as profound prose!

CHARLOTTE. It's beautifully written. Frightening to read, but beautiful.

TOM. No no, it's like the whole of *Pillars*, overblown, discursive, I should have left the wretched book burnt.

CHARLOTTE. Burnt?

TOM. Yes, I burnt the whole thing. Then wrote it out again. Couldn't leave it alone. The book's like a rash all over me, I can't stop scratching it.

CHARLOTTE. But… you wrote it out again after losing it on Reading Station.

TOM. That's right. I lost it at Reading, wrote it from memory, burnt it and wrote it out again. I know I know! It could be seen as an act of grotesque arrogance. I've written my so-called masterpiece three times.

CHARLOTTE. And Daraa was in all three manuscripts?

He looks at her.

From this point in the scene the light begins to slowly increase.

TOM. Perhaps.

CHARLOTTE. How do you mean 'perhaps'?

TOM. I mean, yes. I think so.

CHARLOTTE. You mean you're not sure whether you wrote about Daraa in the previous versions, or not?

TOM. Oh, Charlotte, writing out the book again twice was like automatic writing, it was as if it were being dictated to me.

CHARLOTTE. You mean like Homer? 'Sing, Goddess, of the wrath of Achilles…'

TOM. Yes, 'Sing, Goddess, of the folly of Tom Lawrence…' (*Laughs.*) I'm not comparing myself to Homer.

CHARLOTTE. I would.

TOM. That's because you're kind, and indulgent to me.

CHARLOTTE. Maybe not so indulgent.

A moment.

But in this version, you wrote everything that happened in Daraa.

TOM. Yes.

CHARLOTTE. That really happened.

A moment.

TOM. No.

CHARLOTTE. No?

TOM. Actually it was far worse.

CHARLOTTE. Oh, that's what…

TOM. Sorry?

CHARLOTTE. Nothing, that's what someone thought.

TOM. They were right.

CHARLOTTE. Will you tell me how it was worse?

TOM. I can't do that.

She is offended.

CHARLOTTE. Oh. The beastliness of men's secrets…

TOM. Charlotte…

CHARLOTTE. I need to know.

TOM. You do not…

CHARLOTTE. …I need to know because I am in love with you.

He begins to laugh, stops himself. He is lighthearted.

TOM. That is really not one of the best ideas in the world. Actually, it's one of the worst. You don't know what I am.

CHARLOTTE. Oh, you are obviously a homosexual.

LAWRENCE *does not react.*

What am I, do you think?

He shakes his head.

I am a celibate. Bernard and I don't sleep together.

TOM. Please…

CHARLOTTE. He has actresses for that. I do mind, of course, particularly when the actress is Mrs Patrick Campbell, that minx. But I am utterly devoted to him. There is love on a spiritual plane.

TOM. Far less messy than on an earthly one.

CHARLOTTE. Don't mock me, Tom.

TOM. I would never do that.

CHARLOTTE. Daraa. Tell me what was worse, was it what the Bey did to you in his bedroom?

LAWRENCE, *nothing*.

What the men did to you, after they beat you?

TOM. You must stop asking me, you have no idea…

CHARLOTTE. Or was there something else?

TOM. Charlotte, my dear…

CHARLOTTE. I can help. (*Smiles*.) As a celibate, I can do all kinds of magic.

She takes his hands.

And I think I am the only person in the world you can talk to.

He withdraws his hands.

A silence.

TOM. What was worse, far worse, was that I wanted it to happen to me.

CHARLOTTE. Why?

TOM. Because I deserve to be whipped to death. And thrown away, on a midden. With old bones and waste and excrement.

CHARLOTTE. Oh, Tom, that's… silly, how can you possibly think of yourself like that?

TOM. Because I stink of bad faith! And did, right through the war. I reeked of it.

CHARLOTTE. You can't think so low of yourself…

TOM. I tried to be two things at once: Army Officer and Prince Feisal's friend.

CHARLOTTE. Great men often contain more than one person within them.

TOM. Don't say 'great man', don't talk of me like that, it's a mockery.

CHARLOTTE. You understood the Arab cause. And you could help them because you were a British officer. You got them money and guns, you got Allenby and the British High Command to understand how Feisal could lead the revolt. I cannot see the shame.

TOM. She cannot see the shame. (*Laughing*.) She cannot see. Cannot. See. Cannot. Cannot see, cannot. Cannot. See, cannot, cannot...

CHARLOTTE. Stop, Tom, stop it.

He stops.

A pause.

TOM. I was a spy.

A pause.

I spied on Feisal, I spied on the Arabs.

CHARLOTTE. Spied...

TOM. I was an Intelligence Officer. All the time I was in the desert I sent back report after report to Allenby... what the Arab military strengths were, what Feisal was thinking, the power struggles between the tribes... And... simultaneously, in some kind of inside-out way in my head... I was an Arab freedom fighter! Leading camel charges, under the ragged banners, pistol held high in my fist!

CHARLOTTE. You fought for them.

TOM. No, I betrayed them. I got the Arabs to fight by promising them their freedom. All the time I knew what I was: the servant of an empire that would never let a bunch of camel-fuckers rule their own country.

CHARLOTTE. You are too hard on yourself, you tried to stop the map-drawing, you went to Downing Street, you

denounced British policy to the King's face, you went to the
Paris Peace Conference...

TOM. Paris wasn't a peace conference, it was a conqueror's
banquet, to carve up the Middle East like a fat turkey at
some mad, Christmas dinner... I tried to speak to Feisal in
Paris. He wouldn't even see me. And I can't blame him.

CHARLOTTE. You've done what you could...

TOM. Don't say lame things like that, Charlotte. I've no idea
what I've done. We have no idea, as a civilisation. We may
even have destroyed ourselves.

CHARLOTTE. We'll reap the whirlwind.

TOM. I think so.

The room is now very bright. LAWRENCE *is dead still.*

CHARLOTTE. Why did you lie about Daraa?

A pause.

You lost the book deliberately, didn't you. And then burnt it.
And then when you wrote it a third time, you put in the lie.

A pause.

You wanted to destroy everything you did. Destroy the book,
all record of the desert, disappear. But you couldn't bear it.
People not knowing, not being in the spotlight, the limelight.

A pause.

So you've left it to chance. To be found out. To be disgraced,
utterly destroyed. Or not.

A pause.

A kind of literary Russian roulette?

A pause.

You can't include it in the *Seven Pillars*. It will contaminate
everything, even the victory at Aqaba.

TOM. Daraa was real.

CHARLOTTE. Tom…

TOM. He fucked me in my arse until I bled.

The light in the room is at its brightest.

CHARLOTTE. Tom…

TOM. They beat me until the bone was bare.

CHARLOTTE. Tom…

TOM. It was real.

A beat.

CHARLOTTE. Tom…

TOM. I wanted it. It is real to me, now. It is what I live. Every day.

CHARLOTTE. But it didn't happen.

TOM. I've made it happen. I wrote it.

CHARLOTTE. It's a fiction.

TOM. I told you! It's real.

CHARLOTTE. Tom, admit it, just to me.

A silence.

TOM. It has to have been real. Because of the pain.

CHARLOTTE. But it's a lie.

TOM. There are great truths in lies. I know. I've lived them.

At once the lights snap back to the evening state of the lamps in the room. And LAWRENCE *stands abruptly.*

Look, I think I shouldn't put you to trouble any more, maybe Higgs could telephone for a taxi to take me to Harpenden.

CHARLOTTE. If you think so, of course.

TOM. Thank you for all the work you've done on *Pillars*, and on *Revolt*.

CHARLOTTE. Not at all, but…

TOM. I think they're both in good shape now, don't you?

CHARLOTTE. Do you?

TOM. Oh yes.

CHARLOTTE. All right, Tom.

TOM. You are such a good friend to me, Charlotte.

CHARLOTTE. I do hope so, I do so much hope so.

For a moment they are looking at each other.

Scene Five

Four weeks later.

CHARLOTTE*'s sitting room.*

PATCH – *as in the first scene – sits on a sofa, pen in hand, paper on a board on her lap. She is still.*

SHAW *enters at speed. He stops. He raises a hand dramatically to say something. He freezes.*

Then he turns and exits at speed.

PATCH *sighs.*

CHARLOTTE *enters from the garden. She is wearing a beekeeper's hat and is taking off beekeeper gloves.*

CHARLOTTE. Has he…?

PATCH *shakes her head.*

CHARLOTTE *sighs and takes off the beekeeper hat. She sits and, with a pencil, writes in a notebook.*

Increase in numbers of worker drones… estimate two thousand in hive one, perhaps more in hive two. Queen in hive one continues to produce eggs…

SHAW *enters and immediately begins to deliver.*

PATCH *writes.*

GBS. None of us ever knew what anything meant to her. She was like nobody else; and she must take care of herself wherever she is; for *I* cannot take care of him. Her.

He jams up. And is about to flee.

CHARLOTTE. That is for the epilogue to *Saint Joan*?

GBS. It is…

CHARLOTTE. You do know who you're really writing about?

GBS. To follow dear Oscar, you can only really understand the world by writing of yourself.

CHARLOTTE. Yourself as St Joan as a surrogate for Lawrence of Arabia?

GBS. Who knows? The life force is unpredictable.

CHARLOTTE. If it really exists.

GBS. You were so very fond of Tom Lawrence.

CHARLOTTE. Yes. My choice of men has always been pretty rum.

A beat.

PATCH. Can we just…

GBS (*to* CHARLOTTE). What news from the hives?

CHARLOTTE. Numbers are building up for the spring.

GBS. Bees are a difficult audience, they can swarm at any moment.

CHARLOTTE. You wanted to keep them.

GBS. I will return to hive duty, once *Saint Joan* is finally done.

CHARLOTTE. No, we will beekeep together.

GBS. Ah. Well. I would like that.

CHARLOTTE. So would I.

GBS. Equality in marital stinging.

CHARLOTTE. But to bring forth honey.

They smile at each other.

CHARLOTTE, *closing the notebook and standing.*

I am going to talk to the gardener about extending the wild-flower meadow.

She exits.

GBS. I fear she misses Tom badly.

PATCH. That's not for me to say.

GBS. Why did he leave so suddenly?

PATCH *looks at him.*

Not for you to say.

PATCH *considers for a moment.*

PATCH. All I will say is that I doubt whether we will ever see Colonel Lawrence again.

GBS. That would be a terrible shame.

PATCH. Well, let us hope he has found some kind of peace.

GBS. Fat chance of that. Now, to finally get St Joan to bed, if you get my meaning, I think…

CHARLOTTE *enters from the garden at speed.*

CHARLOTTE. Bernard, Blanche…

SHAW *is about to exit but* PATCH, *looking out into the garden, exclaims.*

GBS. What? Do not say the journalists are coming in over the fields.

CHARLOTTE. No, it's…

She cannot speak.

And LAWRENCE *enters from the garden. He is wearing the uniform of a private in the tank regiment.*

TOM. Hello.

GBS. In the name of sanity, man, what are you wearing now?

TOM. It's a private's uniform. Good, isn't it? Though it is very scratchy. Look, what I've been thinking is, let's finish editing *Revolt in the Desert.*

CHARLOTTE. A private? You're back in the RAF?

TOM. No, no, I've enlisted in the Army, in a tank regiment.

CHARLOTTE. Under your own name?

TOM. Of course not.

GBS. What name is it this time, then?

TOM. Shaw.

He grins.

End play.